Forensic Crime Solvers

Poison Evidence

by **Michael Dahl**

Consultant:
Glenn G. Hardin, MPH, DABFT
Toxicology Supervisor
Minnesota Bureau of Criminal Apprehension
St. Paul, Minnesota

Capstone *press*

Mankato, Minnesota

Edge Books are published by Capstone Press
151 Good Counsel Drive, P.O. Box 669, Mankato, Minnesota 56002
www.capstonepress.com

Library of Congress Cataloging-in-Publication Data
Dahl, Michael.
   Poison evidence / by Michael Dahl.
   p. cm.—(Edge books. Forensic crime solvers)
   Includes bibliographical references and index.
   ISBN 0-7368-2697-1 (hardcover)
   1. Forensic toxicology—Juvenile literature. 2. Poisoning—Juvenile literature. I. Title.
II. Series.
RA1228.D34 2005
614'.13—dc22   2004000209

Summary: Describes the different types of poisons, how poisons affect the body, and how
investigators find poisoning signs at crime scenes.

Editorial Credits
Carrie A. Braulick, editor; Juliette Peters, series designer; Enoch Peterson, book
   designer; Jo Miller, photo researcher; Eric Kudalis, product planning editor

Photo Credits
Bruce Coleman Inc./Lee Foster, 16
Capstone Press/Gary Sundermeyer, 4, 6, 7, 8, 9
Corbis, back cover; Bettmann, 13; Eye Ubiquitous/Edmund Neil, 14; Steve Sarr, 12
David Liebman Quality Nature Photography/David Liebman, 21
Index Stock Imagery/BSIP Agency, front cover; Zefa Visual Media, 19
Mikael Karlsson, 1, 20, 22, 25, 26
PhotoDisc Inc., 29
Steven J. Meunier, 10, 18
Visuals Unlimited, 15

1 2 3 4 5 6 09 08 07 06 05 04

Table of Contents

CHAPTER 1

Learn about:

- Investigators
- Signs of poisoning
- Digitoxin

A Sudden Death

Four friends watched a football game on TV. The Bulldogs were battling the Rockets. Harry and Victor wanted the Bulldogs to win. Dan and Jason cheered for the Rockets.

The friends relaxed in Harry's living room. Chip bags, pizza boxes, and empty soft drink cans littered the room. Harry took a sip of his soft drink. He yelled as one of the Bulldogs' players was tackled. Suddenly, Harry grabbed his chest. His friends thought Harry was joking. But Harry's skin grew pale. His body slumped on the sofa.

Victor reached for his cell phone. He dialed 911. Dan knelt down and felt for Harry's pulse. There was no pulse. Harry was dead.

Four friends gathered to watch a
◀ football game.

Clues

Two emergency medical technicians (EMTs) arrived. One of the EMTs saw small drops of liquid at the corners of Harry's mouth. She called the police.

Soon, three investigators and a medical examiner (ME) arrived. One of the investigators used a cotton swab to collect some of the liquid. The investigator put the swab into a plastic bag.

The ME examined Harry's body. She found no wounds. His skin was pale and cool.

Harry's body slumped on the sofa.

The EMT noticed that liquid was gathered at the corners of Harry's mouth.

The Investigation Begins

The investigators asked the three friends what Harry ate and drank before he died. Jason said they had all been eating pizza and chips. They had been drinking soft drinks. The investigators took some of the leftover food and soft drinks. They planned to send the samples to the police lab for testing.

The ME and investigators placed the body into a plastic bag. They put it on a stretcher. The ME rolled the stretcher to her van and then drove to the morgue.

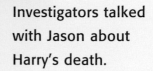

Investigators talked with Jason about Harry's death.

Digitoxin

At the morgue, the ME performed an autopsy on Harry's body. She examined the body to find clues about how he died.

Lab workers tested the samples the investigators had collected. The lab workers found a small amount of digitoxin in one of the soft drink cans. Digitoxin is a chemical in some medicines. People with heart problems often take medicine with digitoxin in it. A large amount of digitoxin can cause people to become sick or die.

The lab workers also tested the liquid on the swab. The liquid was a mixture of stomach acid, half-digested food, and digitoxin. The ME told investigators that natural causes probably did not kill Harry.

Further Investigation

The investigators visited each of Harry's three friends. One of the investigators asked Jason about the day Harry died. He learned that Jason and Harry had bet thousands of dollars against each other on the game.

The investigator looked through Jason's bathroom. He saw a bottle of heart medicine. It contained digitoxin. Based on this evidence, the police brought Jason to the police station.

An investigator found heart medicine in Jason's bathroom.

CHAPTER 2

Learn about:
- Chronic and acute poisoning
- Drugs
- Natural poisons

Types of Poison

Poisons are substances that are harmful to the body. Poisons can be liquid, powder, or gas.

Poisons can kill quickly or slowly. Acute poisons kill people quickly. Chronic poisoning happens when poisons slowly build up to a deadly level.

Household Poisons

Many common household products are poisonous if they are not used properly. About 90 percent of poisonings occur in the home. Some kitchen cleaners contain the poisons sodium hydroxide or potassium hydroxide. These chemicals can break down body tissues.

Many household cleaning
◄ supplies are poisonous.

Illegal drugs such as crack cocaine cause thousands of deaths each year.

Lead is another poison. Lead can damage the skin, eyes, and other organs. Before the 1970s, people often painted their homes with lead-based paint. Today, people no longer use this type of paint.

Drugs

Drugs can be poisonous. Each year in the United States, about 16,000 people die after taking legal or illegal drugs.

Both prescription drugs and drugs people buy without a doctor's order can be harmful. Many people become sick when they do not use drugs properly. Sometimes people become sick if they take too much of a drug.

Illegal drugs include heroin, cocaine, and marijuana. These drugs are dangerous. Many people die when they take too much of an illegal drug. Other people die when they use different illegal drugs at the same time.

Alcohol is another poisonous drug. Many people drink alcoholic beverages. Alcohol can harm the liver. In large amounts, it can cause death.

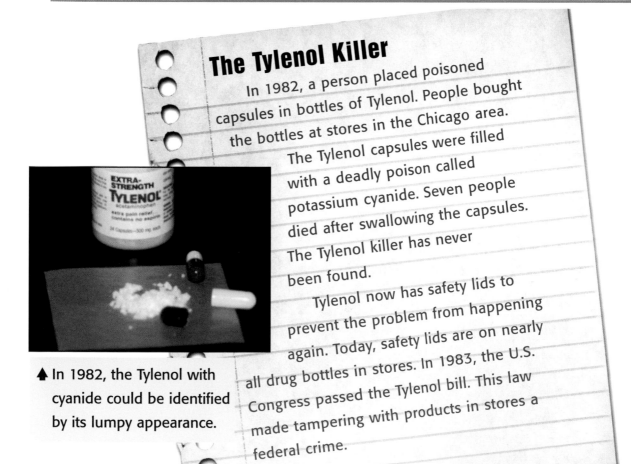

The Tylenol Killer

In 1982, a person placed poisoned capsules in bottles of Tylenol. People bought the bottles at stores in the Chicago area. The Tylenol capsules were filled with a deadly poison called potassium cyanide. Seven people died after swallowing the capsules. The Tylenol killer has never been found.

Tylenol now has safety lids to prevent the problem from happening again. Today, safety lids are on nearly all drug bottles in stores. In 1983, the U.S. Congress passed the Tylenol bill. This law made tampering with products in stores a federal crime.

▲ In 1982, the Tylenol with cyanide could be identified by its lumpy appearance.

Chemicals that farmers spray on crops can put poison into the air.

Environmental and Natural Poisons

Some poisons are in the environment. Asbestos from factories can pollute the air. Oceans, lakes, and rivers sometimes contain mercury. Mercury levels can build up in fish. People who eat fish with high amounts of mercury may become poisoned.

Fluoride is sometimes found naturally in water sources. Some communities add fluoride to their water supplies. Fluoride helps prevent teeth from rotting. But large amounts of fluoride are poisonous. In 1992, more than 260 people in Alaska became sick after drinking water with high fluoride levels.

Some plants naturally produce poisons. The castor-oil plant contains the poison ricin. In 1978, Bulgarian writer Georgi Markov died after being poisoned with ricin. He had been attacked by a man with an umbrella. The umbrella injected a pellet of ricin into Markov.

Ricin is found in the beans of the castor-oil plant.

CHAPTER 3

Learn about:
- Body systems
- Carbon monoxide
- Strychnine

How Poisons Kill

Poisons attack major body systems. Three major body systems affected by poisons are the digestive system, circulatory system, and the nervous system. A person will die if one of these systems stops working.

Digestive System Poisoning

The digestive system includes the mouth, stomach, and intestines. Some kinds of mushrooms poison the digestive system. People who eat amanita mushrooms may throw up, have stomach pains, or die.

Arsenic is a poison that damages the cells of the digestive system. Victims of arsenic poisoning may feel dizzy and weak. In serious cases, arsenic poisoning can cause death.

The death cap and other types of
◄ amanita mushrooms can cause death.

For hundreds of years, people have used arsenic to poison others. In 2003, members of a church in Maine were poisoned when they drank coffee with arsenic in it.

Circulatory System Poisoning

The circulatory system moves oxygen throughout the body. It includes the heart, blood, and blood vessels.

Carbon monoxide is a poisonous gas that attacks the circulatory system. The gas causes the body to run out of oxygen. Carbon monoxide is odorless and colorless. People often do not know they are breathing in the deadly gas.

Carbon monoxide poisoning can happen when vehicles are running in a closed garage.

Arsenic can cause death by damaging the digestive system.

Car exhaust contains carbon monoxide. Cars left running in enclosed places can cause carbon monoxide poisoning. In 1994, Kenneth Westmark was found guilty of murdering his two sons. He placed them in a vehicle that was running in a garage.

Nervous System Poisoning

Some poisons attack the nervous system. This system includes the brain and spinal cord. It sends messages from the brain to other body parts.

Strychnine is a poison that attacks the nervous system. Strychnine affects body chemicals that operate muscles. Victims of

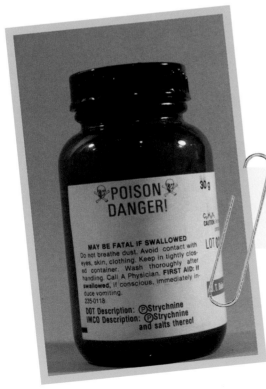

The poison strychnine attacks the nervous system.

strychnine poisoning have muscle spasms. The muscles tighten so hard that they sometimes break bones. After several minutes of spasms, the muscles wear out. Muscles around the lungs stop working. The victim can't breathe and dies. Victims of strychnine poisoning are usually found dead in an unnatural position. Their backs are arched and their eyes are wide open.

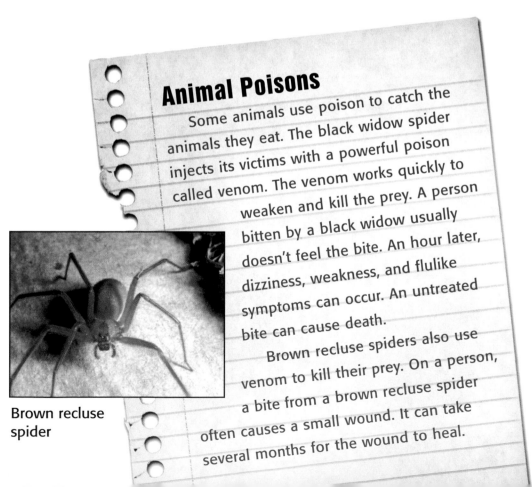

Animal Poisons

Some animals use poison to catch the animals they eat. The black widow spider injects its victims with a powerful poison called venom. The venom works quickly to weaken and kill the prey. A person bitten by a black widow usually doesn't feel the bite. An hour later, dizziness, weakness, and flulike symptoms can occur. An untreated bite can cause death.

Brown recluse spiders also use venom to kill their prey. On a person, a bite from a brown recluse spider often causes a small wound. It can take several months for the wound to heal.

Brown recluse spider

CHAPTER 4

Learn about:
- Crime scene clues
- Caroline Grills
- Lab work

Detecting Poison

Investigators look for poisoning clues at crime scenes. MEs also study dead bodies for signs of poisoning. Each poison leaves behind different clues.

Signs of Poisoning

After a poison enters the body, the body often tries to get rid of the poison. People may throw up. Investigators collect samples of vomit. They place it into plastic bags. They send the samples to a lab to be tested.

MEs look closely at a victim's lips, mouth, and nostrils for signs of poisoning. Potassium permanganate can cause a slight brown coloring inside the mouth and throat. Hydrochloric acid

Investigators look for signs of
◀ poisoning at crime scenes.

or chlorine gas can cause a yellow coloring in the mouth. Swollen lips and blisters near the nostrils are signs that the victim breathed ammonia.

The poison thallium causes a victim's hair to fall out. This clue led to the arrest of Australian Caroline Grills. In the mid-1940s, Grills was found guilty of trying to murder a relative. She had put thallium in the victim's tea.

Investigators pay attention to scents at crime scenes. Cyanide smells like bitter almonds. Victims poisoned by selenium smell strongly of garlic.

Investigators also consider how quickly poisons affect victims. Heroin, ammonia, digitoxin, and mercury usually affect people instantly. Other poisons take more than 12 hours to affect a victim.

Investigators look for possible poisoning sources. ▶

Forensic scientists
often test blood to
find poison evidence.

Autopsies

MEs do autopsies to help them find out how a person died. During an autopsy, MEs closely examine the outside and inside of a body.

The condition of body tissues, internal organs, and muscles may show signs of poisoning. Powerful chemicals can burn their way through the body. Others leave a jellylike substance in the body. Large amounts of painkillers can turn the liver yellow. Fat also can build up around the heart. Victims of cyanide poisoning may have blood or a liver that is bright pink.

Lab Testing

MEs take blood and tissue samples from the body. The samples are sent to a lab. Forensic scientists test for poisons in the samples.

Forensic scientists sometimes use machines to test for poison. Machines can separate, identify, and measure parts of a sample.

Poison and Crime

Clues from a crime scene or autopsy may lead investigators to believe poisoning caused a death. In these cases, they try to decide who caused the death. Some people are accidentally poisoned. Other people kill themselves on purpose. Some victims are murdered.

Good investigators know that clues to a death are not always easy to find. They know about the signs poisons leave behind. Attention to detail can help them find a criminal and solve a case.

Symptoms and Poisons

Chest pain—carbon monoxide, jellyfish venom, sea anemone venom, turpentine

Dehydration—alcohol, amanita mushroom, aspirin

Dizziness—arsenic, aspirin, nicotine, turpentine

Headache—arsenic, carbon monoxide, elderberry, Galerina mushrooms, nicotine

Muscle stiffness—marijuana, strychnine

Stomach pain—amanita mushrooms, ammonia, arsenic, aspirin, cocaine, iodine, mercury

Unconsciousness—carbon monoxide, cocaine, heroin, marijuana, turpentine

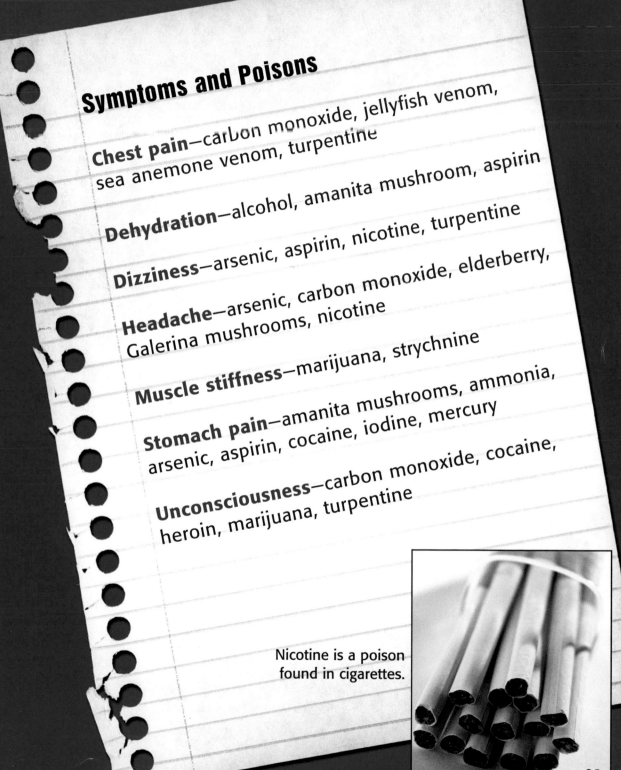

Nicotine is a poison found in cigarettes.

Glossary

arsenic (AR-suh-nik)—a poison that usually is in a gray-white powder form

autopsy (AW-top-see)—an examination performed on a dead body to find the cause of death

carbon monoxide (KAR-buhn muh-NOK-side)—a poisonous gas produced by the engines of vehicles

evidence (EV-uh-duhnss)—information, items, and facts that help prove something is true or false

medical examiner (MED-uh-kuhl eg-ZAM-uh-nur)—a public officer trained to study bodies to find out cause of death

prescription (pri-SKRIP-shuhn)—an order for drugs or medicine written by a doctor

spasm (SPAZ-uhm)—a sudden tightening of a muscle that cannot be controlled

symptom (SIMP-tuhm)—a sign that suggests a person is sick or has a health problem

Read More

Parker, Janice. *Forgeries, Fingerprints, and Forensics.* Crime Science at Work. Austin, Texas: Raintree Steck-Vaughn, 2000.

Platt, Richard. *Crime Scene: The Ultimate Guide to Forensic Science.* New York: DK Publishing, 2003.

Silverstein, Alvin, Virginia Silverstein, and Laura Silverstein Nunn. *Poisoning.* My Health. New York: Franklin Watts, 2003.

Internet Sites

FactHound offers a safe, fun way to find Internet sites related to this book. All of the sites on FactHound have been researched by our staff.

Here's how:

1. Visit *www.facthound.com*
2. Type in this special code **0736826971** for age-appropriate sites. Or enter a search word related to this book for a more general search.
3. Click on the **Fetch It** button.

FactHound will fetch the best sites for you!

Index